"The future of the music does not belong to the major labels. It belongs to the true independents."

André Gray

Muddy Waters was on tour in Europe and a wide-eyed reporter asked him, *"Mr. Muddy Waters, are you a millionaire?"* Muddy looked at the journalist and said, *"No, but all my managers are."*

INTERNET KILLED THE VIDEO STAR

LEARNING RESOURCES
CENTRE

Havering College
of Further and Higher education

ANDRÉ GRAY

TABLE OF CONTENTS

ABOUT THE AUTHOR

André Gray, the inventor of online music sales certifications on a global scale, is the recipient of the highly prestigious Johannes Gutenberg Inventor Prize and the Central America Science Association (CASA) Visionary Award plus an additional 85 awards and counting. Mr. Gray founded DEMO: Digital & Electronic Music Organization, Inc. www.d-e-m-o.com in October of 1999 as a web-based company that gives out online and digital music sales certifications awards on a global scale. He pioneered the business model by being the first person in the world to hand out online music sales certifications awards, thus establishing the globally accepted *de facto* standard. Mr. Gray has been featured in dozens of newspapers and radio programs and is also a seminar and university speaker.

FOREWORD

The turn of the 21st century, which roughly coincided with the digital revolution, was ushered in not in peace and harmony but rather in confusion and strife. As we stand at the threshold of the most anticipated century in history, we are faced with more optimistic technological and creative possibilities than ever before in human history. If harnessed and appropriated properly, the accomplishments of man in the 21st century can seem like a quantum leap into the future that would be limited only by our imagination. The Internet, in all its semantic glory, has collated the disparate countries and continents into one cohesive digital global village and instantaneously signaled the arrival of globalization. This digital revolution has rendered many business models and industries obsolete by placing the power of art, commerce, and science into the hands of the common people. Such is the case of the music industry. This is a very brief treatise on the much written about subject of the digital music revolution. It is important to note that whatever decisions are made in the first two decades of the 21st century will invariably serve as a fairly accurate barometer in determining the outcome for the remainder of the century and perhaps beyond. If this tiny volume can serve as a contributing factor to the confluence of factors that will lead to the empowerment of the common people, then I would be honored. And, while not everyone in the digital age is an artist, at least we have found a means of expression.

André Gray
Inventor of online music sales certifications

MAJOR MISTAKES

When music fans the world over began to download and trade music files by the billions, the major labels, to say the least, were very upset. In true depraved human nature, they began to look at their immediate surroundings to single out the culprits responsible for their sudden and steep music sales decline. At first they pointed to the popularity of free music on the Internet. The only problem with this theory is that there has never been any empirical data to either correlate or substantiate such outlandish claims. The music industry's assertion, as always, was based on fear and ignorance. Next, the industry tried to shift the blame, though more tongue in cheek this time, upon cell phones, movies, the Internet, and the ubiquitous rise and sophistication of video games. While there is some element of truth to the latter statement, the real reason had more to do with the very poor and formulaic quality of music and artists that record companies have been forcing down the throats of the music buying public for many years. One of the first, and perhaps greatest, mistakes that record companies made was their failure or total lack of interest in artists' development. By refusing to place the artists at the epicenter of their operations, they have sent a message to both the rest of the music industry and the record buying public that their myopic view of instant cash is more financially rewarding and important for record companies than, let's say, creating a long-term career vision with the artists that would enable musicians to crystallize their unique vision over the course of a couple of decades while enjoying both critical and financial success without the loss of aesthetic respect from their peers and fans. Perhaps this explains why record companies don't take musical risk and would be more than happy to sign many, if not most, artists whose musical talent and training is no greater than that of William Hung, the rejected would be contestant of the popular television show American Idol. The result is that at least 95% of all musical products released by big record companies have a talent scope and product quality that range anywhere from very bad to truly awful. But, the ringing cash registers were pure music to the executives' and entrepreneurs' ears. Things have gotten so bad that even in Nashville where musical integrity is the number one ingredient for successful country music artists, things have gone awry. In the 21st century, if a country act wants to sing traditional country music in the vein of George Jones or Patsy Cline, that artist would be considered by the decision makers in Nashville to be too *country* for country music. The result is that, for the first time in country music history, the genre has produced many one hit wonders and flashes in the pan that is slowly, but surely, killing traditional country music, as we have known it for almost a century. The objective in Nashville is not to preserve the rich and illustrious tradition of country music but rather to get it while it's hot. This mentality, of course, is a microcosm of the state of the entire music business yesterday, today and, given the opportunity, even tomorrow. So, one might ask, how did the music industry get into such a perilous position? Aside from very trite musical offerings by big record companies, the next logical answer would have to be bad management, very bad management.

Record executives and entrepreneurs in the music business do not necessarily view themselves and their entities with a level head and in a rational manner. Rather, they view themselves as lords of their fiefdom and therein lies the explanation for their irregular business practices and irrational behavior. Many of these entrepreneurs and executives lack the business acumen to function even at an entry level position in, say, the banking or software industry. A brief conversation with many of these senior executives and entrepreneurs would cause one to walk away shaking one's head saying to oneself, "I don't see *how* that person became successful in the music business." If that wasn't enough, the music business, by its very jaded nature, is very incestuous in its hiring and promotional practices. There are more than a few people in the music business who hold lofty positions and take home a very handsome salary not because of their extraordinary talent and accomplishments within the industry, but rather because of who they know or, as in many cases, slept with. What this has done, unfortunately, is to close out prospective people from the music business that may very well have real talent and vision that, given the opportunity, could really make a tremendous contribution to the music business and popular culture. Apart from hiring and promoting the wrong personnel and releasing substandard music, record companies invariably lack any real overall corporate strategy whatsoever. The strategic foundational principles by the likes of Michael Porter and strategic fads like the six sigma are totally alien to these record label managers. The management style of the labels, though blindly sincere, resembles something closer to management by chaos, not strategic vision and planning. What makes the situation even worse is that they have never really tapped into their own creativity by seeking to think outside the box. By thinking outside the box, these executives and entrepreneurs would have spotted new business opportunities, created new and sustaining revenue streams and sought out shorter, better and more economical ways to approach and champion the music business instead of relying upon the same antiquated business models that have been in existence for the past seventy-five years. If record companies were thinking outside the box, or simply just reading the writing on the wall in very big, bold, flashing letters, they would have embraced technology a long time ago as perhaps their best ally, not their greatest foe. History has shown that whenever the music industry embraced technology, the big record companies stood to benefit the most. Radio, as an example, created quite a stir when it first appeared upon the scene; record company managers were arguing that people would not be willing to pay for music that they can listen to for free. As it so happens, ostensibly, that same free radio is responsible for selling records more than all other media combined in the entire history of the music business. No wonder the practice of payola has become such a standard business practice in the music industry with record companies using tons of money, intimidation and, if necessary, just enough violence to virtually control the programming directors' play lists. Video cassette recorders or VCRs, though more related to the movie industry, posed pretty much the same problem when they were first introduced to the consumer market. Movie studios argued that the sale of VCRs to consumers would result in markedly lower box office receipts because consumers would simply wait for the movies to be released on home video. If box office receipts were to take a nose dive, it had nothing to do with the VCR; it may have been a testament to the multitude of bad, predictable and quite forgettable movies that Hollywood has a tendency to churn out. Whether it was because of or in spite of those movies, the VCR, then DVD, gave new life to movies that were stillborn at the box office, provided an elongated life to every genre and sub-genre of films imaginable and went on to become the proverbial gravy of Hollywood's multiple revenue streams model.

A granddaddy of major mistakes of the record companies was the recording contracts that they have been doling out to recording artists since the inception of the music business itself; and, for these industry standard contracts, the devil was, and still is, in the details. These standard recording contracts resemble somewhat a modern day massacre. Even superstar contracts are nothing more than a little bit of cosmetic surgery done to the contract and are still very much disproportionate in their practical application to the artists. Signing a recording contract, with any size record company, is like signing your life away. One of the first rights that signed artists discover very quickly is how little, if any, rights they may have retained. The recording artists don't really have any control over their music, image, likeness and marketing. In fact, many recording acts don't even own the rights to their own names let alone all of their own publishing and master tapes. A clause that is almost universal in all recording contracts, even for superstar attractions, is that the record company is not even obligated to release any records by the act. Then there is a provision that grants record companies the right to give away 15% of artists' recordings under the guise of free goods. In circa 2004, a full length CD had an average manufacturer's suggested retail list price of $15.98 US. If a major attraction were to sell, let's say, 5,000,000 units that would translate into $11,985,000 or 15% of a $79,900,000 retail sales that the record company would not have to share with the artists. In reality, though, the record company does not give away 15% of artists' recordings as free goods. The record company may, at best, give away anywhere from 10,000–25,000 promotional units to radio stations, distributors and retailers as a marketing incentive. The record company accounting books, however, will show that it did give away 15% free goods. But, then again, record companies usually keep several books for practices like these. This, need I remind you, does not include the one to three million units the record company presses up and ships out the backdoor and sells "off the books" for about $3 cash per unit. In true music business lingo, this is called the "cleans," as in clean tax-free profit. After all is said and done and all deductions are made, most recording acts will see only 70 cents per unit out of $15.98. That is *before* all recording budget, marketing, music videos production and promotional costs and other administrative costs are deducted. After that, the manager takes 20% of the recording act's take off the top and the group members share whatever little money, if any, is left. A random examination of any royalty statement from any act from almost any record company will demonstrate that very few artists actually make money from selling records; almost as a rule, most recording acts' earnings are realized from touring, merchandising and performance publishing royalties. Recording contracts are so onerous and capacious in nature that criminal charges ought to be filed against record companies for offering them to unsuspecting musicians. Many people, both inside and outside the music industry, asked how come the business practices and the contracts are so irregular if not downright criminal.

> *Recording contracts are so onerous and capacious in nature that criminal charges ought to be filed against record companies for offering them to unsuspecting musicians.*

The answer to such an inquiry dates back to the very birth of the industry itself when it was built on shaky ground that is predicated upon executives and entrepreneurs taking advantage of the artists. The oppression and exploitation of both the artists and music buying public (by charging exorbitant prices for music) lasted for decades. In order to become successful in the music business, you either had to go through a major label, in one incarnation or the other, or you didn't go at all. It was a frustrating proposition to deal with the record companies but the musicians had no choice. And then, all of a sudden, in 1989 something very miraculous happened. An Oxford University educated computer scientist, Tim Berners-Lee invented the

World Wide Web. When he first invented the World Wide Web, Tim Berners-Lee did not necessarily intend for art and science to be pursued as separate and distinct disciplines but rather as an interwoven tapestry that unleashes humankind's creativity and ingenuity as we investigate the greater mysteries and meaning of our collective existence. The e-commerce dimension that completed the perfect digital troika would be dreamed up by visionary entrepreneurs in the early 1990s. Then people soon discovered that they can send and receive document files over the web. Some of these files were music files and music fans the world over found not only a new way of sharing their enthusiasm for their favorite recording artists but they also found a very cool way to stick it to the music industry for overcharging them for inferior product for many years. The first really big free music website was MP3.com followed by a more decentralized and immensely popular Napster who, in turn, begot many sons of Napster. While there is no way to substantiate exactly how many free musical files were downloaded or traded at the turn of the 21st century, it would be a reasonable assumption to estimate that perhaps the number of files ranges in the billions.

This sparked a very heated debate that quickly saw the formation of two distinct and diametrically opposed schools of thought. The first school of thought postulated that we live in a civilized world and it would be nothing less than barbaric to outright steal art from the artists without any regard for the governing laws of the land that promise everybody life, liberty and some form of fair compensation for our creative endeavors. If continued, they argue, we will become creatively, culturally and morally bankrupt thereby slavishly rendering ourselves to maybe a tentative step above the caveman.

The second school of thought, though less philosophical, believes that even with the billions of supposedly free music files downloaded it still cannot compensate for the billions of dollars that record companies have stolen from the musicians over the last seventy-five years and the exorbitant prices that they have been charging the music buying public for markedly inferior quality music.

This, of course, does not include all the decomposed bodies strewn in the Las Vegas desert or in the back alleys of New York City.

This, of course, does not include all the decomposed bodies strewn in the Las Vegas desert or in the back alleys of New York City. How, they argue, could anyone possibly put a price tag on issues such as oppression, price fixing, black-balled musical careers, intimidation, racketeering, mysterious disappearances, chart rigging, fraudulent accounting and unsolved homicides? PRICELESS!

Facing three consecutive years of a music sales slump, the music industry, led by the Recording Industry Association of America (RIAA) decided to do what is considered by many people to be the dumbest and worst possible thing any embattled industry could do: sue their own customers! Never before in the entire history of industry and commerce have we witnessed such a legal and vituperative

> *In fact, the only thing more spectacular than the rise of the traditional music business is its sudden (and permanent) decline and free fall.*

onslaught directed at 12 year olds, senior citizens, John Does, and, for true absurdity, the deceased. The music industry's Blitzkrieg came down on thousands of civilians like a Junkers JU 87 Stuka blasting its siren signaling financial and legal destruction for those caught in the Stuka's crosshairs. With the music industry electing to sue thousands of music fans, they have once and for all broken covenant with the people and they can never make restitution or come home again. The lawsuits marked the beginning of the end for the traditional music business and all the corruption it entails. In fact, the only thing more spectacular than the rise of the traditional music business is its sudden (and permanent) decline and free fall. Before big music returns to the obscurity, from which they once came, they should be reminded to take their parasitic trade groups along with them because the future of the digital music business does not belong to the majors; it belongs to the true independents.

STEVE JOBS: THE ELVIS OF DIGITAL MUSIC

S teve Jobs has no place in digital music history. Steve Jobs *is* digital music history. This statement is more than a fitting compliment for one of the most extraordinary men in world history who is responsible for creating not one, not two, but three major revolutions. In the mid 1970s he and his business partner, Steve Wozniak, created the computer desktop revolution reducing the cumbersome, bulky computer from the size of a small car into a small, yet powerful, desktop machine that puts computing in the hands of the average person. And, for those technology historians who really want to mark the time and starting point of the computer revolution, the introduction of the Apple Computer is their Plymouth Rock. For his second revolution, Jobs started Pixar Animation Studios that makes digital animation cartoon movies that rendered Disney Animation Studios, both artistically and financially, obsolete. These two revolutions, whether taken into consideration together or separately, are far more than enough to guarantee Jobs a very prominent place in world history. But, in many ways, his greatest legacy may very well be his digital music revolution. When Steven Jobs created Apple iTunes Music Store, he was ahead of his time and, at the same time, he was right on time. Stated differently, and perhaps more succinctly, he was in the right place at the right time doing the right thing thereby capturing that magical and historical moment. There

> *Steve Jobs has no place in digital music history. Steve Jobs is digital music history.*

were, though, other digital music pioneers who came before Jobs upon whose shoulders Jobs proudly and humbly stands.

Long before Jobs became the king of digital music, there was, and still is, a reigning Prince. In 1997 Prince, the Minneapolis based musical genius of geniuses, and the very first major artist to harness the power of the web, released his four-disc CD set titled *Crystal Ball* and sold it exclusively through the web. He sold an astounding 250,000 plus units and the sales figures keep increasing as music fans continue to discover his music. And while it may seem commonplace today for musicians to sell CDs over the web, it was considered quite unorthodox and revolutionary for a major artist to circumvent the so-called major label distribution system and, in the process, realize a much greater artistic and financial freedom that other major artists signed to major labels could only dream of. There was one struggling musician and entrepreneur who sat up and took notice of Prince's web of success. His name was Derek Sivers and he would make the Internet his musical baby.

Struggling as an independent musician to make it in the music business in late 1990s, Derek Sivers started to sell his own CDs to fans through his web based company, CDBaby. Business was so good that he got the idea that instead of selling only his own music, maybe fans might have an interest in purchasing a variety of independently produced music. His hunch paid off. Not only were people more than willing to pay for independent music, they bought so much music that in the fall of 2004 CDBaby announced that they had sold an astonishing 10,000,000 units. This milestone is, by far, the single most impressive success story in digital music this side of Steve Jobs, especially when you consider the fact that practically every act on his roster was a complete unknown. Pundits have pointed to the fact that comparing the sales of CDBaby to iTunes Music Store is like comparing, quite literally, apples to oranges. That may be true but we are talking about 10,000,000 oranges! Who wouldn't want that? But this story is already common knowledge to everyone in the music business. The deeper meaning of this success story confirms the theory that music fans want a variety of authentic, good music that is not the final product of the cookie cutter syndrome that has been forced upon them by Big Music. And yet, for the overwhelming success of CDBaby, Derek Sivers and his company does not garner the level of credit, press coverage and music industry accolades that he so rightly deserves as a true independent operator who instituted a successful new business model. What's worse, when innocuous music industry trade groups promote legal online music stores on university campuses, successful independent music stores like CDBaby and Garageband.com are never even mentioned as a viable option to illegal music downloads. This is ironic because the last thing college kids want, and need, is people forcing trite, uninspired corporate pop music down their throats.

So even though there were pioneers who came before him, everyone agrees that Steve Jobs is the king of digital music. What baffles some people, though, is how come someone else didn't simply lay claim to the throne even before Jobs announced the launch of his iTunes Music Store in the spring of 2003? Sony Corporation, the entertainment behemoth, could have and should have been a runaway success by a mile. Their business model would have resembled a cross between Dell Computers and Apple. They have in their vast portfolio and intellectual capital every possible ingredient and resource. They own movie studios, record companies, e-commerce divisions, music publishing companies, a vast array of high quality electronics, and an ultra successful video games division. Their failure to seek out new business opportunities, synergies within their own company divisions and very poor strategic planning and execution led to their demise. And, in a business world where everyone is thinking and operating in Internet time 24/7 and the global competition encroaches from every corner of the globe, Sony is so far behind that many experts wonder if this tarnished company will ever be able to turn things around. But, given that we are at the start of a new century and the dawn of the information age, if this sleeping giant were to wake up she could become to the Internet what China will be to the world in the 21st century.

While Sony Corporation could eventually position itself to dominate the Internet, if Bill Gates & Co. were to have their way this will never happen. Even though they are late to the portal party, no one who knows the history of technology is willing to hedge their bets against Microsoft. To the casual observer, it seems that the real secret to Microsoft's success is to purposely stand on the sidelines as an observer and let other technology companies release new technology products and seek to develop a market for that product or service that may not have existed before while they work out the kinks. After the technology becomes a run-away success Microsoft then decides if they should enter the market. If Microsoft chooses to enter a particular market, as they usually do, it's doomsday for their competitors. For those people who remember Netscape, WordPerfect and the once popular spreadsheet Lotus 1-2-3, it does show that there is some grain of truth to this late entrance strategy. The company introducing the software will bear the brunt of cost to develop, introduce and market a new product. A company like Microsoft will simply attend the feast that was pre-pared for them by someone else. It should be point-ed out that there is nothing illegal or even immoral about a company that prefers to take a wait and see position. In fact, in an age of very expensive research and development costs, it is a very brilliant strategy, to say the least. It certainly makes a lot of sense. The only thing that is richer and more impressive than Bill Gates' bank account is his immense intellect. If Steve Jobs is considered to be the Elvis of digital music then Bill Gates, who takes a back seat to absolutely no one, considers himself to be nothing less than The Beatles.

If MP3.com and Napster took the music industry by storm, then Steve Jobs is a full-blown tsunami. He didn't start it but it started with him. He stepped in and rescued an industry from the brink of almost total ruination, revolutionized it, and left new benchmarks in the wake of his monumental success. This is the greatest music revolution since the rise of Elvis and the birth of rock

> *If MP3.com and Napster took the music industry by storm, then Steve Jobs is a full-blown tsunami.*

and roll in the1950s. Others who came before him had bits and pieces and showed occasional promise. But, when Jobs came along he became the very essence of digital music embodying all the essential elements the same way that Elvis Presley cultivated the look, stance and voice of rock and roll that has never been equaled. Again like Elvis, Jobs' success and contribution to the music industry is so breathtakingly immense that for centuries to come he will be talked about and written about as the yardstick against which everyone in the future will be measured and no one will likely be able to equal. Even though he is still walking among us, he has already, at least metaphysically, stepped off the pages of business magazines and into the pages of mythology where only fiction writers, poets and great dreamers of the highest order are allowed to write and speak about him in the most sacred and poetic manner. His unique legacy is so intact that any future activity or inactivity, no matter how great or small, cannot diminish his wonderful contribution to the digital revolution.

In order to understand Jobs' greatness, one would have to comprehend the overwhelming odds stacked up against him and the state of the music industry when he first decided to enter the music business. Jobs courageously stepped into a beehive of free digital music downloads that were occurring by the billions each month and bet the farm that people would be willing to pay for the same music they were downloading for free. In a relatively short period of time, the iTunes Music Store sold hundreds of millions of downloads and, in the process, forever killed the traditional major-label-controlled bricks and mortar distribution system and forced the big labels to reconsider their anti-quated and corrupted business model. This success did not come without a price. The shrewd big labels negotiated a music catalog licensing deal with Jobs that gave the labels a very unfair 70/30 split. After the labels, publishers and other music business parasites get their take, iTunes is left with approximately 5 cents from every 99 cents per song sold. It is so blatantly obvious the music industry is taking advantage of the online music stores by taking too large a piece of the pie. To make matters worse, the big labels want to pressure iTunes and other online music stores into adopting the pricing strategies recommended by big music. In the music business, it is a time honored tradition for big music to engage in price fixing, chart rigging and payola. This does not mean, however, big music should be allowed to transmute their cartel practices to the Internet, even though it would be very interesting to see them make an attempt to do so. Online music store operators have the technology and the power to dictate the terms of the business relationship. Basically, big music met their match. Perhaps what record labels need to do is to become more humble in their ongoing relationships with online music stores. Truth be told, it is never the place of record labels to tell or dictate to online music stores how much to charge for music sold or how to operate their music stores. They should simply license their music to online music stores for an agreed upon percentage, which should give the record companies a reasonable 30% with the remaining 70% going to the online music store, especially since the online music stores will have to pay for advertising, marketing, staff salary, legal fees, utilities, office lease and technology costs, among other expenses. Realizing that they cannot afford to get caught up in any federal investigation for price fixing, online music stores, basically, ignored the constant nagging from record companies and continued conducting their business in a professional and honest manner.

In the wake of selling hundreds of millions of downloaded singles, Jobs has also been given the credit, or blame, for killing the album as an art form. Nothing could be further from the truth. Since the birth

> *Most recording artists are actually* **contrived.**

of rock and roll, every decade has produced no more than five or so artists who can create what would be considered, by all accounts, to be a true concept album. Most recording artists are actually *contrived.* They do not play any musical instruments whatsoever and they invariably rely very heavily upon recording studio gimmickry to enhance their awful vocal performances. The simple truth is that most albums released by record companies have one or two formulaic, radio friendly singles and the rest of the album is, quite frankly, nothing but garbage. No other words would suffice. Maybe what the record companies are really trying to say is that they are not impressed with the measly pennies they earn from online music sales; they miss the enormous windfall profits they used to make from the sale of full length CDs, especially over the course of the remaining two decades of the 20th century. So then, the real problem is not the death of the album as an art form, for it was never an art form for most artists. Rather, it is the death of the full length CD as a cash cow, even if most of the songs on the full length CD were less than to be desired, which was usually the case. One must admit, though, that the debate over price fixing and singles versus full length albums seems to pale in comparison to the hot button of interoperability.

With the popularity of secured digital music sales, there came a necessity for digital rights management or DRM. Even in its infancy, controversy surrounds DRM and there are a variety of DRM formats to choose from; and, while the music buying consumers have not started to openly complain about DRM format incompatibility, record companies certainly have. Mr. Jobs, the current market leader of digital music sales by a wide margin, has received the brunt of the criticism for opting not to share his proprietary DRM. In true music business fashion, pundits began their speculation by weighing the pros and cons of Jobs choosing to keep his DRM proprietary for now. If he chooses to share his DRM with other online music stores and MP3 player manufacturers, the playing field would be instantaneously leveled for the competition, which makes absolutely no sense. This also means that both iTunes Music Store and the iPod, the iconic MP3 player, would experience significant sales decline and a loss of market share. Even worse, Wall Street analysts would severely punish the entire Apple Corporation, from which it would be very hard to recover. Now, if Jobs chooses not to share his DRM and decides to keep it proprietary, Apple Corporation is guaranteed to retain its runaway market leadership at least for the remainder of the first decade of the 21st century. But, even so, this would also be temporary and it would be only a matter of time until someone unleashes the iPod killer. And, as many music industry experts are predicting, history could very well repeat itself by Apple gaining the lion's share of the market at the start of a technological boom and as the industry matures they end up as nothing more than an ultra cool but extremely small niche player, as they have been in the past. But, if people were to look a bit closer at this prediction of impending doom they may see a major difference that could possibly point to a very surprising direction in this already amazing story. Apple Corporation makes computers for creative people and they dominate computer sales in the creative arenas. IBM compatible computers were created more for business and academic pursuits, which far outnumbers the creative segment. Stated more succinctly, it was considered more of a necessity than the Macintosh computer; therefore, for the sake of practicality, it would only be natural for IBM compatible computers to dominate overall computer sales by as much as 96% for decades. Entertainment content and gadgets are a want not a need; furthermore, consumers would more than likely have an entirely different perception in their purchasing decisions when it comes to buying a product that is intended for leisure use rather than business or academic use. Now, here is the point. Apple is known and greatly respected for its creative endeavors and products far more than any other technology company and the creative coolness of iTunes Music Store and the iPod is right up Apple's creative alley. Because of this, digital entertainment fans would rather trust the mighty cool Apple Corporation than practically any other company of this era because, if nothing else, Apple wrote the book on techno cool. If this theory is right, Apple may very well become the perennial leader of digital music and entertainment for many decades to come with an occasional serious challenge. After all, when you think of creativity, do you think of Microsoft Corporation or Apple Computers? Without giving this question any thought process, the obvious answer by a thousand miles is, quite naturally, Apple Corporation. With this in mind, Jobs, who keeps his innermost thoughts and future plans for Apple to himself, may have figured this out a long time ago, which explains why he would be reluctant to share his DRM with his competitors and even business partners. It is a brilliant short- and long-term strategy for Apple Corporation. Not content with their inability to dictate and control DRM policy, record company executives, as always, stepped way out of line by asking Jobs to share his DRM with other digital music companies because, according to their weak argument, it would eliminate the speed bumps that are hindering greater music sales. Nonsense. By Steve Jobs opening up his DRM to competitors, record companies would be the only true financial beneficiaries by realizing greater revenue streams from many online music stores while, at the same time, the online music stores would cannibalize each other thereby destroying the burgeoning digital music business in its infancy. For their part, it would be no surprise if big music were to lobby the U. S. Congress and try to have a policy enacted that would make it mandatory for all online music stores to come to some sort of consensus and use a uniform DRM thereby benefiting big music's overall control factor. It's funny, when record companies engage in fraudulent business practices on a daily, if not hourly, basis they certainly don't seem to need the help of Congress. Surely Congress has more important things to think about like national security, outsourcing, terrorism, social security and the national debt than to allocate their precious time to such trivial matters like digital rights management issues. Perhaps the best course of action is to let digital music consumers decide with their voices and, more importantly, with their pocketbooks, which is where the real power resides. But, regardless of the future outcome of the DRM debate, one thing is for certain: record companies should have absolutely no say in its outcome for this decade or any future decade. It is, simply, none of their business.

While still relatively young, Steve Jobs, 50, has lived a very full and mythical life that very few people, if any, will ever have the great honor to experience. He knows what it is like to experience great success and temporary failure, both business and personal. He also knows that there is no greater pain and humiliation that a man can experience than for him to be forced out of a company that he created and built from the ground up.

Always a great learner, he learned a great deal from his past bad experiences and will see to it that those mistakes never occur again. As the veritable Elvis of digital music, Steve Jobs created the template for digital music success and casually deposited it in our minds and told us to grab the knowledge and run. Jobs, much like Elvis, will always be the king of digital music, no matter what. Having said that, Steve Jobs may be considered by most to be the Elvis of digital music but there is one thing that he must never, ever forget: *The Beatles are coming!*

EMANCIPATION OF MUSICIANS

Joseph Schumpeter, the revered early twentieth century economist and astute judge of economic trends, noted that new and emerging companies, especially those introducing new technologies, are better able to sustain the economic well-being of society by eradicating all previous established competitors who relied upon paradigms and technologies that are now considered to be either obsolete, inferior or both. Furthermore, he postulated that industries and even entire countries that elect to protect their incumbent paradigms and technologies were, in effect, deliberately hindering the advancement of technology, industry and the country as a whole. That, in a nutshell, is precisely *the* major problem of the music industry. This thorn in the flesh, which has many dimensions to it, goes far beyond the superficial argument of kids downloading free music from the Internet. In fact, even if there were no free music being downloaded by anyone, the music industry and its trade groups would still have major concerns about a new medium that poses, for the first time ever, a very serious threat to the once mighty distribution system that record companies used to rule with an iron fist. The Internet, with its many interactive possibilities and ease of use functionality, has artificially rendered the once compartmentalized and monolithic music industry totally obsolete by decentralizing and enmeshing the disparate components that were once controlled by major labels and big media holding companies.

It can be said that the same freedom and flexibility that the Internet has provided independent musicians with unheard of empowerment is the same counter force that is destroying big music.

> *Perhaps it is not for the traditionally centralized music business model, or even a radically re-engineered paradigm, to be transmuted to the Internet!*

For the first time in music business history musicians can have both domestic and global music distribution and a direct and interactive relationship with their fans all over the world without the reliance upon any major label or distribution system. Realizing this fact, record companies have been grappling with their biggest problem of how they can transmute their existing music business model to the Internet. This issue, which expands and contracts with every public debate, produces a very poignant, if not painful, point of learning: *Perhaps it is not for the traditionally centralized music business model, or even a radically re-engineered paradigm, to be transmuted to the Internet!*

What this means, as difficult as it may be for big record companies to come to terms with, is that there's no need for major labels anymore. It's that simple. Musicians, after many years of being severely used and abused by major labels, have been emancipated. The first thing newly emancipated musicians should do is to condition their minds that they do not

> *The 21st century musicians' first and greatest victory is to have a full understanding and acceptance of their core articles of faith that lead to their emancipation, as set forth by the liberating powers of the Internet...*

need a recording contract or distribution agreement with a major label in order to become successful in the music business. The 21st century musicians' first and greatest victory is to have a full understanding and acceptance of their core articles of faith that lead to their emancipation, as set forth by the liberating powers of the Internet; this realization, when harnessed and appropriated in the right manner with positive energy, is far more important to both musical success and personal fulfillment than the embracement of all enabling technologies *combined*. The primary objective of musicians, then, should not be to secure a recording contract with big record companies but rather to seek out the many alternatives made possible by the digital music revolution.

The emancipation of musicians will give rise to hundreds of thousands, and eventually millions, of independent and micro record labels. It should not be difficult for independent labels and artists to return to the forefront of the music industry. Independent labels have always been the lifeblood of the music business in terms of introducing new, unadulterated genres and sub-genres of music that have been considered by the music industry to be on the outer fringes of the mainstream market. As major labels took control of these bourgeoning genres, they invariably stripped away their authenticity, watered down the excitement and ultimately reduced the music to nothing more than contrived throwaways that mirror no resemblance or legacy to the genre from which they once emerged. The ubiquitous rise of independent and micro labels will also, undoubtedly, usher in a new era of entertainment Darwinism as creative artists and companies compete for the attention and money of the consumers. But, for those who are technologically savvy and can differentiate themselves from the competition, whether through marketing strategy, competitive pricing, or P. T. Barnum-like gimmickry, the rewards and creative freedom can be great. Therefore, musicians have no more excuses as to why they can't be full-time working musicians. Everything that musicians could ever want or need to help their career advancement in the music business is at their fingertips either for a nominal price or, in many cases, free. The playing field is now level. Big music's far flung, monolithic structures and their expensive recording and marketing budgets were once used as a very high barrier of entry that kept independent musicians on the outer fringes of the music business game. Today, those same attributes are seen as a hindrance in the Internet era where small, creative companies are loose and nimble and can respond to market trends and technological innovations much more quickly than their top-heavy competition that are burdened down in layers of corporate bureaucracy.

The days when recording artists would rely very heavily upon Svengali characters to pull the strings and the artists simply go along for the ride is over. The new order of the day is the artist with a team and no recording contract with big music. The artist's team may consist of, give or take, an attorney to handle all legal matters, an agent to secure live performances, and a manager to manage the day to day operations of the artist's business affairs and to help the artist make important career decisions; other personnel can be added as the need arises. Every artist will, or at least should, own their record label, which gives them 100% ownership of their master recordings, music publishing and merchandising rights. The importance of musicians owning their own domain name is almost as important as owning their music masters and music publishing. In fact, the importance is such that it should be a deal breaker if someone else would like to acquire their domain name as a part of any deal. Furthermore, musicians should never forget that they are the employers of the attorneys, managers and agents. These people work for the artists, not the other way around. In order to successfully manage their team, recording artists will have to become more adept at the business side of the music business instead of just leaving it up to their handlers to stay abreast of the current trends in the business. Musicians must be intimately involved in every aspect of their business dealings and the final word and authorizing signature should always be theirs, not some manager, attorney or agent. Speaking of business affairs, a large portion of the musician's income will derive from business to business or B2B music licensing from sources that include, but are not limited to, motion picture soundtrack, video games soundtrack, television, cable, radio, mobile media, commercials, public performances and the many digital music content providers, online or otherwise. Depending upon how successful the act is, concert performances can contribute just as much or even more than music licensing to the artist's bottom line. And even though the CD will die an eventual death, it is quite likely that it will still be limping along, in one form or another, for the first fifteen years of the 21st century. Having said this, and depending upon the genre and the technological sophistication of the audience being catered to, CDs still have a very vibrant life on the Internet and the format still has the ability to produce windfall profits, for now. Independent musicians can still choose to use this format without having to worry about anybody frowning down upon them. Eventually, though, all music delivery over the Internet will be intangible and ubiquitous like mercury.

The emancipation of musicians also marks the end of Top 40 radio as we know it, which is the single greatest thing to happen to the music business since the rise of the Internet and the demise of big music. Long controlled by the music industry cartel, it was next to impossible for independent musicians to get their music on reporting radio stations that really mattered. For many decades, big music, via the radio stations, virtually dictated exactly what listeners would hear and there was nothing that anyone could have done about it. With thousands of records being released each year, radio programming became highly competitive as everyone from unsigned artists to superstars jockeyed for a position.

If independent musicians were not signed to a big record company nor had some sort of direct, or indirect, distribution agreement with them, then radio stations' programming directors wouldn't even meet with these independent musicians, let alone add their music to the play lists. The digital revolution has brought with it a radio revolution that spawned satellite radio, digital radio, Internet radio and podcasting, the Internet era's version of amateur radio. Radio may be sending mixed signals to the music business cartel, but it could potentially become a great friend to independent musicians. And, musicians now have an infinite number of outlets and radio channels that are more than willing to play their music free of charge. Realizing the importance of radio as a great music sales generator, it would be of no surprise to anyone if the music industry cartel seeks to gain control of these new radio incarnations either through policy or strong-arm tactics. Music will become a wonderful mixed bag of everything from indigenous sounds from every continent to more somewhat recognizable sub-genres finding their way onto the airwaves. As musical consumers, our minds will be broadened sociologically, politically, and most importantly, cross-culturally. This will greatly reduce polarization, racism, ethno-centrism and fears that are based upon half truths and downright assumptions. In its place will be a higher tolerance level for cultural diversity, more open communication and a new appreciation for the brotherhood and commonality of the global village we call home that was made possible by the Internet; and, because the digital music revolution has leveled the playing field for musicians the world over, the best and most diverse music this world has ever heard is yet to come. A lot of great music will, in all likelihood, come from Europe. Europeans have always been more open-minded and accepting toward many different types of musical genres and sub-genres not only from Europe but also from the United States of America. In fact, it is the Europeans, not the Americans, who have kept American roots music alive, in one form or another, throughout the last century and will continue to do so. Their eclectic musical taste and insatiable appetite for music consumption will eventually cause them to topple America in digital music sales. China, India and other Asian countries will also collectively surpass America in digital music sales. This time, though, the majority of Asia's music consumption will be homegrown or primarily regional, not American popular music.

Since musicians, professionals and amateurs alike, have more creative freedom and instant global distribution more than ever before, major labels are in serious jeopardy. Corporate pop's irreversible countdown to extinction has officially begun. These so-called major labels will, for an indefinite period of time, be able to participate in, but not dominate, the digital music business. Therefore, music lovers from around the world should no longer refer to them as major labels. In the decades to come, there will be volumes of books analyzing the days of when so-called major labels ruled the music business. Who cares? They are now irrelevant, ancient history. A large part of their undoing was the mistake of firing the wrong employees and executives who may have had real talent and vision. It is these same former employees who were once a part of the big labels' inner machinery and know how the business really works that will go off and start Internet based music companies where they can channel that same unique vision they've had for years while working for a big record company and, in the process, help to vengefully put their former employers out of business. Also, recording artists who were once signed to big record companies and somehow found themselves unceremoniously dropped from the record company because of creative differences or poor record sales will be able to finally create the type of music that they, not the record company, really like and use their celebrity status to sell their music over the Internet. Because many of these recording artists already enjoy some degree of notoriety, they can enjoy stupendous success and carve out a very long career that would have otherwise been impossible. This, need I remind you, is perhaps a best case scenario. It will not be long before the trend of superstar attractions who are signed to big record companies choose not to extend their contracts when it's time for contract renegotiations and choose instead to enter into non-exclusive contracts with many digital music service providers, thus maximizing every possible revenue stream.

As musicians and entrepreneurs migrate to the Internet, they must always proceed with enthusiasm, creativity and extreme caution, lest they forget the hard lessons learned from the first Internet bubble burst that caught many unsuspecting entrepreneurs and investors off guard at the turn of the 21st century. Needless to say, hundreds of billions of dollars were lost. Whether or not they were paying close attention to the e-commerce events of that brief but exciting era, there are many online music stores that are in for a rude awakening. Their mistake, and a major one at that, was to simply copy the iTunes Music Store business model. It seems that almost every other week companies are announcing that they are getting into the digital music download business. Many of these companies have given absolutely no thought process whatsoever to their business models, let alone any real revenue generating plan, which will explain the impending major shakeout that will occur before the end of the first decade of the 21st century. Depending upon whose numbers you want to believe, in circa 2004 Apple iTunes Music Store held a market share of anywhere from 70% to 85% of the digital music download market. What this means is that there are many online music stores that are not making a profit. If the truth were to be told, there are many online music stores whose sales figures are so miniscule that they are either too embarrassed to release their real sales figures or, as in many cases, they grossly inflate their sales figures to impress their online competitors and the rest of the music industry. Apple iTunes Music

Stores considers itself a loss leader and the real profits are derived from the sales of the iconic iPod, its portable MP3 music player. Many online music stores, borrowing a page from Apple's playbook, decided to adopt the exact same business strategy. Despite their already legendary status, Apple's impressive market dominance for both its iTunes Music Store and the iPod cannot and will not last forever. The question then is not if someone is going to release an iPod killer but simply a question of when. This is why it is imperative for all online music stores to operate as a stand alone profitable entity. But, for many of these stores, turning a profit seems to be a very frustrating proposition. The realization of financial success for online music stores as a stand alone profitable business entity need not be overly complex or elusive. The real secret to financial success for online music stores, if it can be called a secret in the first place, is firmly rooted in independent music. It is only after the widespread acceptance of independent music over trite corporate pop as the dominant and preferred choice of music by consumers will online music stores operators be in a position to negotiate fairly with independent musicians and finally turn a tidy profit, thus justifying them being in the music business. When independent music sales rule the Internet, it is then, and only then, that online music store operators will be in a secure position to tell corporate pop exactly where to stick their music.

THE RIAA'S GOOD QUALITIES

THE DIGITAL GLOBAL LEADER

Globalization

When musicians were emancipated by the Internet, they were given almost unlimited powers and possibilities within the confines of the law in regards to what they can do in their quest for finding the perfect nexus by mixing technology, commerce, and art. But, as with all things that are great or truly groundbreaking, there is something required in return. In this case, and within the context of the music business, the requirement is that musicians are no longer expected to be uninformed or dumb. Those days, though filled with some fun and mixed emotions, are long gone. We have migrated from the industrial age to the information age where everyone and everything is expected to be smart, or at least that's the assumption. We have knowledge workers in the work force, smart kitchen appliances and many smart gadgets. Anybody, regardless of race, religion and socio-economic standing that desires to live and compete in the world today will be required to have some marketable knowledge. Musicians are no exception to this universal rule. Emancipated musicians are now saddled with the responsibilities of being a master negotiator, diplomat, effective communicator, technologist, banker, team leader, quasi-attorney, social activist, musician, entrepreneur and martyr. Musicians must be all these things at the same time while they embrace the long awaited globalization. Musicians, as well as everyone else in the world, must realize that our participation in globalization is not an option nor is it escapable by instinct or choice. Therefore, everyone will be required to have a global perspective as a part of our education and social contract with society. Globalization is no longer just a buzz word or a pie in the sky ideology taught to MBA students in graduate business schools.

> *Therefore, everyone will be required to have a global perspective as a part of our education and social contract with society.*

We now live in a globally transformed world where outsourcing, e-mail, real time information, e-commerce, Internet, telecommuting, Intranet and global markets are the order of the day. Instead of team members hoarding knowledge to themselves as in the past to capitalize on the mantra "knowledge is power," we are now in an era where the sharing of knowledge and information is a major way of displaying true knowledge and being a team player. The constant need for new and relevant knowledge has led to lifelong learning instead of just ending one's education upon the successful completion of a bachelor's or master's degree that was so prevalent in the industrial age. These same knowledge workers no longer view their arch rivals as competitors but rather they seek to foster mutually benefiting networked alliances that would produce win-win situations. People of the digital age no longer just work the exact requirement of 9 to 5 workdays. Knowledge workers of the digital age have replaced 9 to 5 with 24/7 as a way to merely keep up with the ever changing world we live in. Perhaps this explains why the virtual office, mobile media and anytime, anywhere has forever sidelined the ball and chain of office buildings as the only or primary place of conducting business. To these high energy achievers, job security is primarily based upon performance and intellectual capital value to the company and industry as a whole, not seniority. The motivating factor for these smart workers goes beyond the scope of just earning a decent salary in order to take care of their families. The motivating factor for these people is ownership, which gives them a certain sense of responsibility and emotional attachment to their job description and the company that they have a stake in. This is the same mentality that has smart workers being more concerned about being a part of a team instead of a union. Many of these companies that employ these knowledge workers will, in one capacity or another, be involved in outsourcing, the new driving force of globalization.

The controversial 20th century economist and primary exponent of the (Paradox of) Comparative Advantage, David Ricardo, argued in 1917 that it is in the best economic interest of a country to import certain goods from another nation when it cannot produce those items as inexpensively as the other nation. Ricardo, along with some of his most ardent and radical followers, even went a step further asserting that it may be to a country's advantage to import goods from other nations even if they have the ability to produce those same goods less expensively at home. The justification for this theory is based upon the premise that by choosing not to produce the item in favor of producing another item, from an economies of scale standpoint, offers better production efficiencies that will benefit both countries ultimately. And so the 21st century globalization began, not in peace and harmony but in turmoil and confusion that will most certainly guarantee the improbable rise of some poor but smart nations to the level of being superpowers and the incomprehensible fall of once invincible nations. In terms of being a superpower, the 20th century belongs to America, and no one would argue differently. In the 21st century, however, that's a different story. There is talk about Japan, India and Indonesia but China is poised to take the whole damn show. This should be of no surprise to anyone because the highly respected British historian, Arnold Toynbee, warned us about this sleeping giant a long time ago. No one questions China and India's rise to become superpowers. What many people wonder about, sometimes out loud, is how other countries that are superpowers will respond to these new superpowers. Usually in circumstances like these, there is tension that sometimes involves strained trade relations, power struggles, turf wars, rumors of war, jealousy and military conflict that erupt out of one country picking a fight just for the sake, or fun, of it. Whatever the seismic changes that globalization will bring to the reshaping of the world and the redistribution of wealth, one thing is for certain: everyone in the world will have to have a global perspective and the necessary tools and knowledge to navigate the highly complex labyrinth of roadblocks, issues and concerns that affect our global village.

Outsourcing

Interestingly enough, outsourcing, a key driver of globalization, will serve to create three distinct categories of countries in the 21st century and beyond: Manufacturing countries, Distribution and Marketing countries, and Consumer countries.

Manufacturing countries: Manufacturing countries will concentrate primarily upon research and development and the manufacturing of goods. Many of these countries that fall into the manufacturing category will be third world countries that boast an incredible arsenal of intellectual capital and streamlined manufacturing capacity that is second to none. Countries in this category will quite naturally dominate other intangible services like customer service, technical help desk, and financial services, which include stock trading. These countries will use their new found wealth and power to lift themselves out of poverty. And because they are also conducting most, if not all, of the research and development, they will seek to take the next logical step and patent their R&D findings. This can be a very sensitive subject matter for the companies from first world countries who commissioned the manufacturing in the first place. The manufacturing countries will have the ability to manufacture goods and develop software in one third the standard time and at ten percent of the cost. They will be able to produce goods in all four consumer categories of quality: low (cheap), medium (average), high (high quality) and exclusive (very expensive). These countries can, and will, sustain themselves with many of the goods that they manufacture and import goods from other nations as needed.

Distribution & Marketing countries: Many of the corporations that choose to outsource their manufacturing of goods are headquartered in first world countries. The reason they choose to outsource their research and development and manufacturing is to realize greater profit margins. In their opinion, they can save anywhere from 80% to 90% on production costs which adds a considerable boost to their financial bottom line objectives. Also, they make a very persuasive argument that they won't have to worry about large staff wages, retirement benefits and unemployment insurance. By outsourcing their manufacturing, these corporations are free to focus their energies upon the fairly complex logistics of supply chain management, distribution and marketing. In short, these corporations that were once considered to be complex living organisms have been reduced to little more than a storefront sales company. Countries that are in this category are in a very vulnerable position of losing their standing as a first world country or as a superpower. At a glance, it seems to make good business sense for the companies outsourcing some, or most, of their work but it can be potentially very perilous for the citizens, in terms of job security and consumer confidence, of that first world country. If outsourcing is not properly managed, it can have devastating long term-economic effects upon the citizens, and eventually the corporations, of those first world countries.

Consumer countries: Of the three possible categories that a country can find itself in, the category of consumer countries is, hands down, the worst category to be in because the distribution and marketing countries that are supplying them with goods can literally control the supply and demand pipeline, thus manipulating the economic and political circumstances of the entire country. Countries that find themselves in this category should seek to transform themselves into manufacturing countries where the only real cost to become a manufacturing country will be intellectual capital. The longer these countries languish in consumer country purgatory, the longer they will remain the dumping ground of distribution and marketing countries, and it doesn't get any lower than that.

The Digital Global Leader Toolkit

Apart from having a very astute global perspective, everyone should seek to develop their leadership skills that go far beyond the national or hemispheric scope, regardless of one's profession. Having in one's leadership toolkit the necessary global leadership skills is perhaps the greatest way to distinguish yourself from your competition and gain the competitive advantage. Listed below are six essential ingredients that every emerging global leader should have in the leadership toolkit. These skills, when harnessed in their full power, can help emerging global leaders to perform their jobs more effectively with verve and intelligence.

Think Globally: The dawn of the 21st century, which roughly coincided with the digital revolution, has forged a trend of strengthened globally connected markets. Leaders will no longer just see themselves as citizens of a particular country but rather as citizens of the world. And, as citizens of the world, leaders must have a better understanding of the political, legal, economic and cultural laws and their ramifications. In the wake of e-commerce and global trade, thinking and conducting business globally is no longer an option; it is a mere requirement just to remain in business. This means that in order to achieve the competitive advantage, emerging global leaders will have to learn to successfully manage outsourcing and foreign production, and international marketing and sales teams in their quest for a piece of the global pie. The secret to achieving the competitive advantage, then, rests in the ability of emerging global leaders to lead across global cultures. Surprisingly, the generic leadership profile has few differences in them, which means that the digital world is more cohesive than we had originally thought. What this means is that the days of narcissistic ethno-centrism are over and will no longer be tolerated. Also, the days when America sneezes and the rest of the world catches a cold are definitely over. Emerging global leaders of the future will actually live or spend a significant amount of time in foreign countries, very much unlike leaders from the 20th century. The exportation trend of white collar workers will be made possible by the Internet whereas software developers in China or Romania can interact with their clients in, say, Brazil in real-time almost as if they were there in person. For the emerging global leaders who can successfully manage across cultures, the future of 21st century commerce belongs to them.

Customer is King: In the previous century, merchants always maintained that the customer is king; but, in reality, it was nothing more than a condescending gesture to appease complaining customers. Not anymore. If the industrial age was the era of customer lip service then the information age is the era of golden glove customer service. Customers of the 21st century have very exacting standards and they want information and products 24/7 anywhere, anytime at Internet speed. In order for companies to be successful today, they will have to place the customer at the epicenter of their operations.

That is, the whole company should be designed and built around the customers' needs and be nim-

> *If the industrial age was the era of customer lip service then the information age is the era of golden glove customer service.*

ble enough to change along with the times. They need to keep in close contact with the customers and find out exactly what are their needs and wants. No matter how large a corporation is and how far their global operations may span, each customer must be treated as a distinct individual with requests for goods and information that need to be delivered immediately and there is no room for mistakes, not even honest ones. In the end, all commerce advancement or reversal in the 21st century will hinge upon the quality of customer service that companies provide to their customers.

Think Long Term: Quarterly reports are, by far, the worst and most destructive thing that ever happened to corporations. It is, to say the least, a very unfair proposition for everybody involved. Shareholders and corporate directors place too much pressure upon chief executive officers and the rest of the senior management teams to meet quarterly financial projections. Let's face it, three months, or even six months, is not enough time to accomplish any real operations, marketing or financial objectives. Also, while corporations in America place a very heavy emphasis upon quarterly financial results, foreign companies, especially those in Asia and certain parts of Europe, have a tendency to focus more upon long term strategy. On many occasions, newly hired CEOs inherit ailing companies with inferior quality products and poor financial performances. In situations like these, it can take many months, possibly years, to turn things around. These CEOs, however, are shown the door within a relatively short period of time if they don't work their magic quickly enough. This has led some people in the business world to finally realize that placing too great a premium upon quarterly financial results makes everyone uptight and uncomfortable in the workplace and impedes their overall creativity and job performance. In other words, it permeates the entire corporation with a very adverse effect; but, stockholders and corporate directors aren't the only ones to blame. A large portion of the blame should be placed squarely upon the shoulders of Wall Street. Wall Street has a tendency, and a very flippant one at that, to severely punish companies that fail to meet their financial projections, even if the companies are in the middle of a turnaround strategy. For some people, though, the problem is even bigger than Wall Street; in terms of influence on the financial markets and the global economy, the chairman of the Federal Reserve Bank wields immense power. The chairman of the Federal Reserve

> *...the chairman of the Federal Reserve Bank has been historically imbued with too much power to the point where every word is regarded as holy scripture.*

Bank is a very special post that should be reserved for only the brightest economists in the world. Whoever holds the chairman's post deserves to be respected and his or her opinion should be of value. Having said that, the chairman of the Federal Reserve Bank has been historically imbued with too much power to the point where every word is regarded as holy scripture. That's the problem. No one man, no matter who he is or what lofty position he may hold, should be entrusted with the power to single-handedly determine the financial and economic fate of billions of people around the world simply by giving his opinion. Just imagine trillions of dollars can be gained or lost based upon one man's skewed but educated guess. A good alternative scenario would be for the chairman of the Federal Reserve Bank to brief the President of the United States of America and the U.S. Congress in private and then the President decides, with the voting approval of the U.S. Congress, whether or not to raise interest rates.

The only way American corporations can migrate from the focus of quarterly reports to long term strategy is for both Wall Street and corporations to agree to discontinue the quarterly reporting system in favor of more substantive long term strategies. Under this new agreement, corporations would still prepare quarterly financial reports but they would not be released. The annual report will be a collection of all four quarterly reports along with other important documents.

Embrace Technology: Even though most executives are not technologists and they do not understand the arcane aspects of their information technology systems, they are required to have a rather keen understanding of how technology can fit into the overall strategy of the corporations they lead, thus maximizing the company's competitive strategy. And, as the company ventures off into electronic commerce, as every company of the 21st century will, leadership and technological skills will become intertwined and cannot be separated as a basic requirement in order to be considered a true leader. For the many future leaders who were raised with technology as an integrated part of their lives in the information age, the transition to leadership will be much easier than for many present day leaders who still lack even the most basic understanding or interest of how to harness and leverage technology as a way of getting a leg up on the competition. While future leaders do not have to be gifted computer whiz kids like Bill Gates, they do need to successfully evaluate and manage investments in new or essential technology, be a technology evangelist leading the entire organization by example of how technology can help them better accomplish the company's objectives and develop a technology savvy work force. Having a leader who is not technologically savvy is to forfeit the competitive advantage within one's industry.

Invest in Intellectual Capital: In the industrial age a company's physical assets were used as a yardstick to measure the value of a company. Today, the most valuable asset that a company has is its intellectual capital. For those who still do not know, intellectual capital is the sum total value of an organization's employees which includes everyone from the senior management executives to regular staffers. We are now living in a really smart society where the value of employees to a corporation far exceeds that of the company's tangible assets and intellectual property, which includes patents, trademarks, and copyrights. There has never been a generally accepted accounting principle rule to accurately reflect the true value of knowledge workers on a corporation's balance sheet. But, for those who do, the values of these corporations can sometimes range well into the billions, as in the case of companies like Microsoft Corporation and Dell Computers. Many of these corporations have developed full fledged in-house universities that rival the very best teaching offered by the top business schools in the world. Life-long learning is not only looked upon favorably, it is now merely a requirement in the business world today. Perhaps this explains why executive training and highly specialized certificate programs are much more preferred by job recruiters and organizations than an MBA degree that came from anything less than a top 20 business school. If information technology is the engine that will drive the corporations of the 21st century, then the intellectual capital will serve as its nitrogen.

Think Outside the Box: The recent catch phrase "think outside the box" may be the latest lingo in the business world lexicon at the dawn of the 21st century but it has existed under different, loosely defined pseudonyms for decades. In short, to think outside the box simply means to think creatively. It brings to the table an unconventional way to problem solving that most other people would have not considered. It is an uneven mixture of art and science with a heavier emphasis on the former. This means that there are no absolutes or one right way to accomplish tasks when it comes to problem solving. That's what makes thinking outside the box unique in the first place. Emerging global

> *...thinking outside the box is even more important than what is popularly known as formal higher education.*

leaders of the 21st century will have to think on their feet in Internet time and approach problem solving from a creative standpoint. If a leader wants to inspire her entire organization to think outside the box, the first thing she will have to do is eradicate bureaucracy by deemphasizing the legalistic approach to the chain of command of the organizational charts. By killing bureaucracy and downplaying the importance of the organizational charts, organizations can unleash a free flow of information and creative ideas that will result in more happy, loyal employees and even happier customers, which means healthier financial statements. In the end, those who master the creative art of thinking outside the box will find that they have a significant competitive advantage over their competitors; in fact, to take it a step further, thinking outside the box is even more important than what is popularly known as formal higher education.

THE GESTAPO'S
MASTER PLAN

✦ ✦ ✦ ✦ ✦ ✦ ✦ ✦

RIAA is the Greatest Hindrance to Technological Innovation

In the court of public opinion, the RIAA is the single greatest hindrance of technological innovation and advancement in the music industry. The lethal venom that they have spread throughout the music industry has served as a severe crippling paralysis that, if left unchecked, will definitely ruin whatever is left of the crumbling music business and suffocate the once inalienable right to freedom of artistic expression. At the heart of music fans' argument is a very onerous and controversial document called the Digital Millennium Copyright Act or DMCA. The DMCA, which originated as a white paper in 1994 in the U.S. Department of Commerce and had a working title of "Intellectual Property and the National Information

Infrastructure," was originally rejected by the U.S. Congress. For some unknown reason at the time, Congress chose not to pass an administration bill that incorporated some of the features of the white paper. Not easily deterred by temporary defeat, the Commerce Department decided to propose some of the features of the white paper to the World Intellectual Property Organization (WIPO) as a part of a negotiation package that led to the 1996 Copyright Treaty. The Commerce Department did this under the assumption that an international treaty, if successfully ratified, would serve as an encouragement to the U.S. Congress to pass confirming legislation. The WIPO, in their astute wisdom and foresight, rejected the proposals and so the Commerce Department decided to work on Congress again. This time, however, they were successful. Signed into law by President Clinton in October 1998 as a response to the WIPO Performances and Phonograms Treaties and the Copyright treaty, the ninety-four page DMCA incorporated those two WIPO treaties into a larger copyright act; the DMCA was divided into five sections as follows:

> *In the court of public opinion, the RIAA is the single greatest hindrance of technological innovation and advancement in the music industry.*

Title I: "WIPO Copyright and Performances and Phonograms Treaties Implementation Act of 1998." This incorporates the treaties from WIPO, a United Nations special agency.

Title II: "Online Copyright Infringement Liability Limitation Act." This provides online service providers with limited liability or 'safe harbor' for some of their activities. From a theoretical standpoint, online service providers are considered to be mere *conduits* of the copyrighted material posted online and it would be cost prohibitive, if not impossible, to monitor hundreds of millions of data files that are posted on the bulletin board services. Online service providers are considered immune if they do not interfere with copyright owners' standard technical measures and if they make a conscientious effort to implement reasonable policies that call for the termination of service for people who infringe upon the copyrights of others.

Title III: "Computer Maintenance Competition Assurance Act." This grants permission to make a copy of a computer program by activating the computer for repair or maintenance purposes only.

Title IV: There are six miscellaneous provisions in all pertaining to topics like distance education, the functions of the Copyright Office and the exceptions in the Copyright Act that are applicable to libraries and for making 'ephemeral recordings' etc…

Title V: "Vessel Hull Design Protection Act." Just as the name suggests, this title provides vessel hulls with a new form of protection when they are being designed.

This is the Digital Millennium Copyright Act presented in a pre-digested and basic framework. Who would have thought that the DMCA, which appears to be an undeserved gift handed to big media on a silver platter, would lead to such consternation in the music, then film, industries? For some music industry trade groups, the DMCA is their treasured *Mein Kampf* upon which they will hinge all their broken dreams in a last desperate attempt to justify their relevance in a decentralized industry that no longer belongs to the so-called major labels that they fought so hard to protect.

One of the most frustrating and disturbing aspects of the DMCA is that it is suffocating technological innovation at an astonishing rate. If continued, we would forfeit the great technological innovations that the 21st century promises us. The computer and software revolutions, for example, would

> *For some music industry trade groups, the DMCA is their treasured* **Mein Kampf** *upon which they will hinge all their broken dreams in a last desperate attempt to justify their relevance in a decentralized industry that no longer belongs to the so-called major labels that they fought so hard to protect.*

have never taken place if the DMCA were around in the 1960s and 1970s. Innovation in its purest and most vibrant form has always been based upon open source or derivative works movements where copyright and bureaucratic obstacles are held to a minimum. As a brief case study, the Beginners All-purpose Symbolic Instructional Code or BASIC programming language was originally developed in 1964 by professors John Kemeny and Thomas Kurtz at Dartmouth College as an easy way for non-computer science majors to learn how to program. By the 1970's when the personal computer explosion began, BASIC served as the impetus that drove the computer manufacturers to provide their own versions of BASIC with titles like QuickBASIC, QBASIC, Microsoft BASIC, GW BASIC and BASICA. Now, if the DMCA were in place back then, technologists would not be allowed to change a single line of code in an attempt to create their version of BASIC. As a second example, VisiCalc, the first truly effective computer spreadsheet, was developed at Massachusetts Institute of Technology by two students only to be later used as an inspiration by inventor Mitch Kapor who went on to create the Lotus 1-2-3 spreadsheet for IBM Corporation. Microsoft would then use Lotus 1-2-3 as a springboard to create the derivative Microsoft Excel spreadsheet and render Lotus 1-2-3 obsolete. Once again, if the DMCA were in place in the late 1970s, Mitch Kapor would have never been able to legally create a derivative work of a copyrighted material. But, if these first two examples were not sobering enough, perhaps the third example of a brief history of the Internet and the World Wide Web should do the trick.

In the late 1960s, the Advance Research Projects Agency, a government affiliate with the Defense Department, created ARPAnet for the transmission of important documents in a more efficient manner. The system was, by its very design, redundant so that it would have many different paths of data delivery so that in the event that one part was not available other pathways could be found easily. It wasn't long before universities and other commercial companies from countries around the world began to use ARPAnet, a precursor to the Internet. In fact, the ARPAnet traffic was so heavy that the National Science Foundation stepped in and assumed the responsibility for providing the backbone services. Realizing by its rapid growth that users would be willing to pay for access to the ARPAnet, private telecommunications companies stepped in and filled the void by providing quicker access to what is now known today as the Internet; but, it didn't stop there. In 1989, Tim Berners-Lee, a researcher at CERN, the particle physics laboratory close to Geneva, Switzerland, created the World Wide Web and its accompanying HyperText Markup Language (HTML). Now, to repeat again, if the DMCA were around in the late 1960s, universities and commercial companies would have not been allowed to change anything on ARPAnet, which means it would have probably never evolved into the Internet and Tim Berners-Lee would have never legally had the opportunity to invent the World Wide Web. So then, the driving force behind the computer revolution and eventually the Internet revolution was an open source commune that was built upon the solid foundation that sharing technology and information leads to greater innovations and technological breakthroughs. This proves that the open source pioneers and evangelists like Frank McLuhan, the great media convergence visionary, Lee Felsenstein and Richard M. Stallman, open source's most famous exponent, were right all along.

RIAA, the Self-Appointed Gatekeeper of the Internet

The RIAA, whatever you may say or think about them, has a far greater interest in the Internet and its governing laws than any other trade group or entire industry for that matter. The RIAA and the record companies that they represent do not necessarily view the Internet as a level playing field where independent musicians and entrepreneurs can legally compete side by side with big record companies. They view themselves as the self-appointed gatekeepers of the Internet who will determine who conducts music business on the Internet, to what extent and at what price. They feel so left behind in the wake of the digital revolution that they are practically insisting upon having a major say in the development of all recording and playback technology. Ideally, the RIAA would love for the Federal Communications Commission

(FCC) to grant them the power to take a sneak peek at technologies and products that are under development, which would give the RIAA the immense control over when, how, and where people listen to music. For a trade organization to assume such power is not impossible. Take, for example, the Motion Picture Association of America (MPAA). In the summer of 2004 the MPAA coerced technology companies like Microsoft and RealNetworks to remove truly innovative features from their latest media software programs that would have made it possible for television viewers to make legal copies of TV programs and transmit them over the Internet to a very limited number of devices including the office, another home or a car. The RIAA is not too far behind the MPAA. The RIAA claims that they do all these things and filed thousands of lawsuits against music fans in the name of protecting the musicians' copyrights. The central issue, they assert, is the blatant violation of copyrighted material. They set forth the argument that whenever music fans copy music off the Internet, they are, in essence, stealing money from the musicians. Nonsense. Big media companies, especially those in the music business, have always used creative artists as a scapegoat in their public debates in an attempt to win public sympathy and to try to pull the veil over the eyes of Congress in order to get legislation passed that would swing in the favor of big record companies. It is common knowledge that record companies look for every possible opportunity to rip off musicians. When music fans copy music off the Internet they are really stealing from record companies, not artists. Everybody knows that musicians see very little, if any, money for the music they have sold. For the first time in the music business, the big thief is being stolen from. Perhaps this explains why 99.99% of all

> *It is common knowledge that record companies look for every possible opportunity to rip off musicians.*

recording artists signed to so-called major labels never publicly commiserated with the record companies or the RIAA. If the RIAA were so concerned about the rights of the musicians, why didn't they sue the big record companies for engaging in the criminal practice of incessant and predatory price fixing? If the RIAA were so concerned about the rights of musicians, why didn't they sue the record companies for engaging in the illegal practice of payola? If the RIAA were so concerned with about the rights of musicians, why didn't they sue the record companies for engaging (influencing) in rigging musical charts? If the RIAA were so concerned about the rights of the musicians, why didn't they sue the record companies for "deliberately" stealing billions of dollars in royalties from recording artists? If the RIAA were so concerned about the rights of musicians, why didn't they sue the record companies for selling millions of "cleans" CDs out the backdoor for cash thereby cheating both the Internal Revenue Service and musicians out of untold of wealth? If the RIAA were so concerned about the rights of the musicians, why didn't they sue record companies for bootlegging their own records? If the RIAA were so concerned about the rights of the musicians, why didn't they sue the attorneys and their law firms and have these attorneys permanently disbarred for cheating musicians out of their money to the tune of millions of dollars? If the RIAA were so concerned about the rights of the musicians, why didn't they sue the many record distributors for selling tons of independent music and then closing down their distribution companies without paying a single penny to anyone only to go into business the next day right across the street? The answer to all these questions is very simple: *You don't bite the hand that feeds you!*

RIAA Stifles Academic Research

Apart from being the self-appointed gatekeepers of the Internet, the RIAA also seem to have a great interest in research. In the spring of 2001, Edward W. Felton, a computer scientist at Princeton University, decided to take part in a contest sponsored by, of all people, the RIAA. The contest was to test technology that is supposed to guard music against piracy. After finding some flaws in the antipiracy software, Felton and his team announced that they would publish their results. When the RIAA was made aware of Felton's intentions, they threatened to sue him under the Digital Millennium Copyright Act or DMCA. Faced with the possibility of a countersuit from Felton, the RIAA eventually backed away from the situation. Fortunately for Felton, the DMCA created specific language to block hackers but made special provisions for researchers to carry out what is considered to be important work that could actually improve the technology in question. This story sent shockwaves throughout the tech community sending a message to many scientists that research takes a backseat to copyright protection. While some people will agree that the music industry does have a right to protect themselves against illegal file sharing, the precautionary steps taken to prevent illegal practices also proves to be a severe hindrance to technological innovation. To many people in the technological community, this scenario is seen as intimidation and could very well deter future research scientists from exploring the unlimited possibilities of technological research and innovation.

DMCA 2.0

Some legal scholars question the onerous composition of the Digital Millennium Copyright Act. There are other legal scholars who would question the very legality of the DMCA. The original DMCA was a gift to big media companies that was handed to them when no one was really paying any attention. It was intended to catch independent media companies off guard by those involved in its creation and ratification. The DMCA places the future of media in the digital age firmly in the hands of the big media companies while it deliberately seeks to freeze out independent media companies. The DMCA is so layered with disproportionate provisions that augur in favor of big media that it should be declared illegal and thrown out. The process should be started all over again with the creation of the DMCA 2.0. The only stipulation this time around is that big media companies and their innocuous trade groups would not be allowed to participate in the drafting of the new DMCA 2.0.

Quite naturally, there are plenty of laws from the original DMCA that would not make it into the new version and there are new provisions proposed for the DMCA 2.0 that were deliberately left out of the original version. The following suggestions are by no means a complete list of everything that would be included in the new DMCA 2.0. It is, however, a starting point.

> ***Reformed Copyright Laws:*** The dawn of the 21st century has seen a great techno-logical revolution and, with few excep-tions, everything changed with it. The copyright laws of the United States of America are one of those few exceptions that didn't change. The old DMCA makes it very obvious that they will stifle technological innovation to the benefit of the big media companies. The new DMCA 2.0 copyright laws would have a more relaxed approach to copyright laws by allowing people to make derivative works of the original copyrighted works without the permission of the original copyright holder. It would also seek to limit the exclusive copyright holder own-ership to maybe 25 years with no exten-sions. It would restore the *Fair Use Doctrine* that is very much missed in the

old DMCA. If all these proposed changes were successfully passed into law in the new DMCA 2.0, it would spark a great technological renaissance of research and innovation that would unleash all the great possibilities that this century promises to offer.

Internet Radio Friendly: The old DMCA has set forth what is considered by many independent Internet radio broadcasters or webcasters to be very suffocating and exorbitant stipulations under which they can operate. The real reason for these stringent provisions is to deliberately discourage all aspiring Internet radio broadcasters. Big music knows very well that traditional radio has always been the best and most effective way to promote and sell records. Before the Internet became popular, big music controlled radio programming through payola which included tens of millions of dollars in cash, illicit drugs, expensive gifts, vacation trips, prostitution, intimidation, and graphic violence. There are very few records, if any, that make it into the top 40 without some form of payola involved. If independent musicians can have their music played on thousands of Internet radio stations, this would translate into hefty record sales for the independent musicians and the end of traditional radio as we know it. So, in order to resuscitate whatever is left of traditional radio, big music made sure that certain provisions were included in the old DMCA to guarantee that Internet radio will never get off the ground in a big way. The new DMCA 2.0 would give webcasters a free reign over their play lists, audience reach, and all performance rights fees would be tantamount to that of ASCAP, BMI, and SESAC. There would be no special appointments of any nonprofit performance rights organizations by the Library of Congress, thus ensuring fair competition among competing companies. Instead of paying a blanket fee for broadcasting rights, Internet and satellite radio stations would be required to pay for only the songs that they actually played. And, with the technological capabilities of the digital era, paying for only the songs you use will eventually become the standard.

Department of Justice, Music Industry Special Task Force Division: If all the media were like children in a classroom, then the music industry is the ornery one that needs extra supervision to make sure she doesn't hurt herself or anyone else in the classroom. The wall-to-wall corruption in the music business is such that the Department of Justice should give serious consideration to the possibility of creating a permanent task force division to keep a close watch over the entire music industry. Needless to say, the Justice Department would always have a very heavy workload with runaway music industry practices like payola, price fixing, many unsolved homicides, music chart rigging, death threats, extortion, fraudulent accounting practices, record companies bootlegging their own records and other predatory business practices. By making sure that the playing field is always level, the Justice Department could end up being independent musicians' best friend this side of the Internet.

CONTACT INFORMATION

www.d-e-m-o.com

Phone: 212-252-2359

Fax: 212-591-6526

DEMO
André C. Gray
244 5th Avenue, #C292
New York, NY 10001-7604

For reordering information please
call **1-800-253-9315**.